BELIEVE
IN THE
WORLD

BELIEVE
IN THE
WORLD

Wisdom for Grown-Ups
from Children's Books

AMY GASH and ELISE HOWARD

ALGONQUIN BOOKS
OF CHAPEL HILL 2024

Published by
ALGONQUIN BOOKS OF CHAPEL HILL
Post Office Box 2225
Chapel Hill, North Carolina 27515-2225

an imprint of Workman Publishing
a division of Hachette Book Group, Inc.
1290 Avenue of the Americas
New York, NY 10104

Printed in the United States of America.
Design by Steve Godwin.

The publisher is not responsible for websites (or their content)
that are not owned by the publisher.

For permission to reprint these excerpts, grateful acknowledgment is
made to the holders of copyright, publishers, or representatives named on
page 143, which constitutes an extension of the copyright page.

Cataloging-in-Publication Data is available from the Library of Congress.

ISBN 978-1-64375-553-3 (hardcover)

10 9 8 7 6 5 4 3 2 1

First Edition

No book is really worth reading at the age of ten which is not equally (and often far more) worth reading at the age of fifty . . .

—C. S. Lewis, *On Stories, and Other Essays on Literature*

CONTENTS

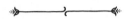

Foreword by R. J. Palacio   xi

Introduction: Believing Again by the Authors   xv

ONE: How to Be Good in the World   1

Kindness   3

Acceptance   8

Courage   12

Confidence   17

Forgiveness   22

TWO: How to Be Joyful in the World   25

Delight   27

Books and Stories   31

Eat, Drink, and Be Merry   37

Indulgence   41

Adventure and Imagination   45

Sense and Nonsense   49

Song and Dance   55

THREE: How to Be Strong in the World   59

Sorrow   61

Fear   67

Defiance   70

People Are Complicated   74

Individuality   78

FOUR: How to Be at Home in the World   83

Family   85

Friendship   89

Community   93

Animals   98

Nature   103

FIVE: How to Believe in the World   107

Optimism   109

Love   112

Perseverance   116

Becoming Who You're Meant to Be   120

Choices   124

Change   129

Faith, Hope, and Possibility   133

Acknowledgments   141

Permissions   143

Index of Books and Authors   145

FOREWORD

R. J. PALACIO

"WORDS. THEY'RE JUST WORDS."

That's what a well-meaning teacher once told me in elementary school after she overheard someone—who I thought was my friend—say something mean to me. "Sticks and stones may break my bones but words can never hurt me," the teacher was trying to tell me, but even at the age of eight, I knew that wasn't always true. Words can hurt. And sometimes, they do.

Of course, the opposite is true, too. Words can heal us. They can lift us up. Inspire. Make us wonder and dream. Words can unite people, move us to see beauty, create, feel. Words, when used to these lovely ends, can arguably be the most magnificent lifters of the human spirit there have ever been. It's language, that almost magical mix of words, sounds, gestures, and symbols, that gives voice to our thoughts and ideas and memories and stories—and was the beginning of our human capacity for wisdom. From generation to generation, wisdom has been passed down through words; from these words, experiences are remembered.

For those of us in the children's book world, it's no secret that some of the greatest pearls of wisdom in all of literature can be found in books for children. It may be because authors writing for children understand their audience well, and know that the number one rule with kids is this: you have to be truthful. There's no room for BS in children's literature. You can't hide behind a literary turn of phrase or a well-written opening line. Kids don't really care about all that. What they really want is the truth, the whole truth. And that's exactly what the best children's books give them. Sometimes, sure, the truth is given lightly, gingerly, covered with a little joke or spoken by a furry creature. Truth can be doled out with a spoonful of sugar, delivered by way of extraordinary adventures and fantastical worlds, or dressed up in princess gowns. Truth skips down school hallways and plays football, and is occasionally quite ordinary. But the best children's books, no matter to what genre or age group they belong, offer readers a connection to truth—and that is the first step on the journey toward wisdom.

I intensely remember the feeling of being completely lost in a book as a young reader, in a story, in the flood of words that created a world in which I belonged. And as an adult, pieces of those worlds still live inside me. They helped make me who I am. They prepared me for life, for adulthood and all that future stuff I couldn't even imagine back then, which is why it's those very stories from my childhood that bring such illumination and comfort to me now—stories and lessons I still turn to today for wisdom. Illumination and comfort are what we all need right now. The more chaotic the world feels, the more we have to believe in that very human power of illumination and comfort, and in our ability to pass those things on to our fellow mortal beings.

Believe In the World reminds us of what we are to one another and what we can give to each other. Light. Wisdom. Love. Goodness. Cheer. By bringing together, in one glorious volume, some of the greatest and most memorable quotes from the wonderfully diverse world of children's literature, *Believe In the World* is nothing short of hope, writ large, for readers of all ages.

INTRODUCTION

Believing Again

NOT SO LONG AGO the two of us found ourselves feeling out of sorts. We were busy with what grown-ups are busy with these days and there never seemed to be enough time. We had hit a wall. Then one of us picked up the collection of children's book quotations that Algonquin had published in 1999 called *What the Dormouse Said* and happened upon this line: "Thou hast only to follow the wall far enough and there will be a door in it."

It turns out that for us—as for so many others—the door was children's books. After going back to Marguerite de Angeli's 1949 *The Door in the Wall*, we were immediately inspired to start collecting the quotations for this new volume. It was time, we realized, to update and expand *Dormouse* for a new century. Over these last twenty years there has been a surge of thrilling new books from a growing diversity of creators who have given us new insights into what it means to be human.

As we read our way through these gems and shared great lines with each other, our spirits began to soar. "There's something wonderful about a present before it's unwrapped. Anything could be inside," Elise texted Amy, paraphrasing Alice in Kevin Henkes's *Junonia*. Amy texted back that she'd forgotten that particular kind of excitement. Sometimes as we worked, we were compelled to take breaks and have snacks. Who could resist after reading that chocolate "is what laughing tastes like" in Katherine Applegate's *Home of the Brave*. It does. One of us may have had some bread and jam, like Frances. Elise returned to French language classes; and Amy, admittedly no dancer, found herself considering tango classes after she read Nicola Yoon's *Instructions for Dancing*: "Not everybody can dance good, but everybody can dance." That's a life lesson that speaks to all of us, young and old.

Of course, the wonderful thing about children's books is that they explore the entire human condition—the good, the sad, the silly, and even the ugly. As Isaac Bashevis Singer wrote in *Stories for Children*, "children ... are highly serious people." These vital stories reflect kids' lives and prepare them for the struggles they will inevitably encounter. And they remind grown-ups that how we respond to what life throws in our path is what really matters. If you're obsessing about that mistake you made in the office, you have Jewell Parker Rhodes to point out that we "can't undo wrong," but we can "do our best to make things right." If you're annoyed with your partner, it can help to read that no one is perfect. "Every human being who loves another loves imperfection," as Susan Cooper knew when she wrote *Silver on the Tree*.

Which is not to say that change is impossible, it's just that "Change takes time. And patience. And . . . a willingness to listen to people we may not understand," as Brandy Colbert writes in *The Voting Booth*. We live in a polarizing era. Maybe giving a children's book to someone with whom you disagree—politically or personally—is a start. It certainly beats dismissing them, and, as Tae Keller makes clear in *When You Trap a Tiger*, "Story magic is powerful, powerful enough to change someone."

Books we read as children imprint on us in ways large and small; they are written, after all, by adults with a remarkable ability to tap into something essential about seeing through the eyes of a child. We could not include in this little volume all the original, hilarious, wise, and powerful authorial voices from all the brilliant children's books we read. Organized by subject, the quotations in this book are printed exactly as they appeared in their original form, which is why you'll notice some quotations are set in italics, some have quotation marks, and others don't.

We hope you'll rediscover some of your favorite titles here, read a familiar line in a new way, or find a fresh children's book to treasure.

Our dream is that *Believe In the World* will remind grown-ups that though we may have wildly different experiences in life, there are plenty of values we all share. Being courageous, speaking out against wrongs, honoring our individuality as well as our differences, being kind and doing good deeds, respecting other points of view, and maybe even breaking a few rules now and then—these are ideals that can bring us together.

These stories represent the world we once believed in—and can again. For us, living with these words has been exhilarating—here's to staying young at heart forever!

"How will you begin?" asks Louisa May Alcott's Charlie in *Rose in Bloom*.

Start by turning the page.

—*Amy Gash and Elise Howard*

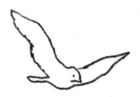

BELIEVE
IN THE
WORLD

ONE

How to Be Good
in the World

Children's books show us that there is nothing more important than kindness. From there, all else flows: the ability to accept ourselves and others—no matter our differences—and the courage to forgive.

Kindness

To be careful with people and with words was a rare and beautiful thing.

—BENJAMIN ALIRE SÁENZ,
Aristotle and Dante Discover the Secrets of the Universe

*What a difference it can make when you treat
another person with simple respect and dignity,
the same respect and dignity you want for yourself.*

—JULIUS LESTER, *Day of Tears*

No kindness is ever wasted, nor can we ever tell how much good may come of it.

—NANCY FARMER, *The Sea of Trolls*

This is what kindness does, Ms. Albert said. *Each little thing we do goes out, like a ripple, into the world.*

—JACQUELINE WOODSON, *Each Kindness*

♥

"You ain't got nothing to back you up 'cept what you got in your heart."

—WALTER DEAN MYERS, *Scorpions*

♥

"The more you give, the more you have. It is the only true thing I know."

—KELLY BARNHILL, *The Ogress and the Orphans*

♥

"I can't *abide* people who go soft over animals and then cheat every human they come across!"

—DIANA WYNNE JONES, *Castle in the Air*

"Though there may be times when your
hands are empty, your heart is always full,
and you can give things out of that—warm
things, kind things, sweet things—help and
comfort and laughter."

　　—FRANCES HODGSON BURNETT, *A Little Princess*

♥

"If you make happy those that are near, those that are
far will come."

　　—GRACE LIN, *Where the Mountain Meets the Moon*

"Shall we make a new rule of life from to-night:
always to try to be a little kinder than is necessary?"
—J. M. BARRIE, *The Little White Bird,*
or Adventures in Kensington Gardens

❦

"Tía Rosa didn't want her kindness returned.
She wanted it passed on."
—KAREN T. TAHA, *A Gift for Tía Rosa*

❦

your smile is not owed
to any man—genuine
compliments are free
—ZETTA ELLIOTT, *Say Her Name*

❦

"Altruism," he concluded, "is the kind of pie best
eaten with a lot of gravy and little inspection of the
kind of kidney it's stuffed with."
—M. T. ANDERSON, *The Kingdom on the Waves*

The thing I realize is that it's not what you take,
it's what you leave.
—JENNIFER NIVEN, *All the Bright Places*

♥

"You saved me once, and what is given is always
returned. We are in this world to help one another."
—C. COLLODI, *The Adventures of Pinocchio*

♥

There is an Arabic proverb that says:
She makes you feel
like a loaf of freshly baked bread.

It is said about
the nicest
kindest
people.
The type of people
who help you
rise.
—JASMINE WARGA, *Other Words for Home*

Acceptance

"Every human being who loves another loves imperfection, for there is no perfect being on this earth—nothing is so simple as that."
— SUSAN COOPER, *Silver on the Tree*

Happiness is wanting what you have.
— PHYLLIS REYNOLDS NAYLOR, *Achingly Alice*

"We can't always do what we want in life . . . so we do the best we can."
— BEVERLY CLEARY, *Ramona Forever*

He didn't ask you no questions about why you weren't this or that. He just let a person be. He let a person sit and think out loud sometimes, and . . . well . . . that's a mighty good thing to do.

—JERDINE NOLEN, *Harvey Potter's Balloon Farm*

"You must let what happens happen. Everything must be equal in your eyes, good and evil, beautiful and ugly, foolish and wise."

—MICHAEL ENDE, *The Neverending Story*

As hard as it is to change yourself, it's even harder to change someone else.

—LISA YEE, *So Totally Emily Ebers*

There comes a time when you're losing a fight that it just doesn't make sense to keep on fighting. It's not that you're being a quitter, it's just that you've got the sense to know when enough is enough.
—CHRISTOPHER PAUL CURTIS, *Bud, Not Buddy*

✗ ✗ ✗

"Living with uncertainty is like having a rock in your shoe. If you can't remove the rock, you have to figure out how to walk despite it. There is simply no other choice."
—AMY TIMBERLAKE, *One Came Home*

It has been a terrible, horrible, no good, very bad day.
My mom says some days are like that.

—JUDITH VIORST, *Alexander and the Terrible,*
Horrible, No Good, Very Bad Day

"It is the way of life. It ends."

—MALINDA LO, *Ash*

"Gotta realize that who you are is all you got."

—SHARON FLAKE, *The Skin I'm In*

Courage

"Bravery doesn't always look like you think it will. And it's never too late to stand up for the right thing."

—BRANDY COLBERT, *Little & Lion*

"If you dare nothing, then when the day is over, nothing is all you will have gained."

—NEIL GAIMAN, *The Graveyard Book*

"Starting is the most difficult part."

—KEVIN HENKES, *Olive's Ocean*

I give you the strength to fight, but you all must learn
the strength of restraint.

—TOMI ADEYEMI, *Children of Blood and Bone*

Make your choice, adventurous Stranger;
Strike the bell and bide the danger,
Or wonder, till it drives you mad,
What would have followed if you had.

—C. S. LEWIS, *The Magician's Nephew*

"It is much *easier* to be brave if you do not know
everything."

—LOIS LOWRY, *Number the Stars*

"Making choices even when they scare you because
you know it's the right thing to do—that's bravery."

—AISHA SAEED, *Amal Unbound*

"But think about how it feels when your hands are so cold they go numb. How it's only when they start to thaw out that you realize how much they hurt."

—LAUREN WOLK, *Wolf Hollow*

"A scar is a sign of strength . . . The sign of a survivor."

—LAURIE HALSE ANDERSON, *Chains*

"If we wait until we're ready we'll be waiting for the rest of our lives."

—LEMONY SNICKET, *A Series of Unfortunate Events, Book the Sixth: The Ersatz Elevator*

"Sometimes a champion is the one who is ready to act, not the strongest or the bravest."

—LAURENCE YEP, *City of Death*

"At night our fear is strong . . . but in the morning, in the light, we find our courage again."
—MALALA YOUSAFZAI, *I Am Malala: How One Girl Stood Up for Education and Changed the World*

"Live courage, breathe courage and give courage."
—DHAN GOPAL MUKERJI, *Gay-Neck, the Story of a Pigeon*

I think everything is happening all the time, but if
you don't put yourself in the path of it, you miss it.
—GAYLE FORMAN, *Just One Day*

Hoping,
I'm starting to think,
might be the bravest thing a person can do.
—JASMINE WARGA, *Other Words for Home*

Confidence

Be bold.
Be brave.
Be beautiful.
Be brilliant.
Be (your) best.

—RENÉE WATSON, *Piecing Me Together*

※ ※ ※

There's no shame in being strong, and there's no one way to be strong. Strength is about being true to yourself and your values . . . Take ownership and pride in the things that make you who you are and who you want to be.

—KELLY JENSEN,
Here We Are: Feminism for the Real World

Never let anyone
lower your goals.
Others' expectations
of you are determined
by their limitations
of life.
The sky is your limit, sons.
Always shoot
for the sun
and you *will* shine.

—KWAME ALEXANDER,
"BASKETBALL RULE #3," IN *The Crossover*

You can't control how people look at you, but you
can control how far back you pull your shoulders and
how high you lift your chin.

—ELIZABETH ACEVEDO, *With the Fire on High*

"You might as well learn right now, you two, that the poorest guide you can have in life is what people will say."
—MAUD HART LOVELACE, *Heaven to Betsy*

❀ ❀ ❀

"Just because you don't know everything don't mean you know nothing."
—KAREN CUSHMAN, *The Midwife's Apprentice*

❀ ❀ ❀

"Never do anything by halves if you want to get away with it. Be outrageous. Go the whole hog. Make sure everything you do is so completely crazy it's unbelievable."
—ROALD DAHL, *Matilda*

❀ ❀ ❀

People nearly always know the right answers, they just like someone else to tell them.
—CAROLINE RUSH, *Further Tales of Mr. Pengachoosa*

"The thing to do is, once you've bloomed,
hold on. Just simply hold on and don't let go.
There one is and there one stays."
— RUSSELL HOBAN, *The Marzipan Pig*

❄ ❄ ❄

Trust dreams.
Trust your heart,
and trust
your
story.

— NEIL GAIMAN, *Instructions*

❄ ❄ ❄

"How will you begin?"
"Do my best all round: keep good company, read
good books, love good things, and cultivate soul and
body as faithfully and wisely as I can."
— LOUISA MAY ALCOTT, *Rose in Bloom*

❄ ❄ ❄

WOO HOO! YOU'RE DOING GREAT!
— SANDRA BOYNTON, *Woo Hoo! You're Doing Great!*

Forgiveness

"That's one of the things we learn as we grow older—how to forgive. It comes easier at forty than it did at twenty."

—L. M. MONTGOMERY, *Anne of the Island*

A girl shouldn't hold a baked stuffed onion against a boy forever.

—BEVERLY CLEARY, *Fifteen*

"We don't forgive people because they deserve it. We forgive them because they need it—because *we* need it."

—BREE DESPAIN, *The Dark Divine*

"Dumbledore says people find it far easier to forgive others for being wrong than being right."

—J. K. ROWLING,
Harry Potter and the Half-Blood Prince

I want to be the kind of person who can do that. Move on and forgive people and be healthy and happy. It seems like an easy thing to do in my head. But it's not so easy when you try it in real life.

—SUSANE COLASANTI, *Waiting for You*

"When you have hurt people, you must allow them their anger. Otherwise it will only become another thing you have tried to take away."

—CASSANDRA CLARE, *Chain of Iron*

"One can never go back. One always has to move forward."

—LIBBA BRAY, *A Great and Terrible Beauty*

maybe I'll never find it in my heart to forgive him. And maybe there's nothing wrong with that, either.

—AMBER SMITH,
The Way I Used to Be

"A mistake made with good in your heart is still a mistake, but it is one for which you must forgive yourself. "

—LINDA SUE PARK, *When My Name Was Keoko*

A heart can grab hold of old wounds and go sour as milk over them.

—CATHERYNNE M. VALENTE, *The Girl Who Fell Beneath Fairyland and Led the Revels There*

TWO

How to Be Joyful
in the World

Goof off. Be silly. Read a book. Tell a story.
Eat chocolate or stand on your head if you feel like it.
Whyever not? Children's books give us permission
to discover what makes us happy.

Delight

─────⟡─────

"Let the wild rumpus start!"
　　—MAURICE SENDAK, *Where the Wild Things Are*

❧❧

The teacher taught me the word in school. I wrote it in my book. B-E-A-U-T-I-F-U-L. *Beautiful!* I think it means: something that when you have it, your heart is happy.
　　—SHARON DENNIS WYETH, *Something Beautiful*

❧❧

Sometimes gay, kind laughter is the best help of all.
　　—FRANCES HODGSON BURNETT, *A Little Princess*

Sometimes the world feels all right and good and kind of like it's becoming nice again around you. And you realize it, and realize how happy you are in it, and you just gotta laugh.

—JACQUELINE WOODSON, *Peace, Locomotion*

∽⌒∾

"Joy is a fragile thing, my boy, and must be treated as such. Too harsh and it disintegrates. Rush, and it disappears."

—KWAME MBALIA,
"THE GRIOT OF GROVER STREET," IN
Black Boy Joy

∽⌒∾

"This day will never, no matter how long you live, happen again. It is exquisitely singular."

—NAOMI SHIHAB NYE,
I'll Ask You Three Times, Are You OK?

How much slower the work went when the joy of it was gone.

—LINDA SUE PARK, *A Single Shard*

"You need a reason to be sad. You don't need a reason to be happy."

—LOUIS SACHAR,
Sideways Stories from Wayside School

I focus my mind and energy on doing things that make me happy like laughing, joking, eating, and spending time with friends. The more I think about it, the more I realize that there really is no other way to live.

—SHANE BURCAW, *Laughing at My Nightmare*

Books and Stories

Books to the ceiling, books to the sky.
My piles of books are a mile high.
How I love them!
How I need them!
I'll have a long beard by the time I read them.
  —ARNOLD LOBEL, "BOOKS TO THE CEILING," IN
Whiskers & Rhymes

There is nothing more luxurious than eating while
you read—unless it be reading while you eat.
  —E. NESBIT, "THE AUNT AND AMABEL" IN
The Magic World

I go home
and help fold the sheets
and peel the carrots and
potatoes and onions
and go sit on the back porch,
covering my toes with a quilt,
and read
to be
another
me.

—NIKKI GIOVANNI, *A Library*

Books make people quiet, yet they are so loud.
—NNEDI OKORAFOR, *The Book of Phoenix*

*It's going to be okay. I'll make friends, and if I don't,
I'll borrow books from the library.*
—KELLY YANG, *Front Desk*

There is no bond like the bond of having read and liked the same books.
—E. NESBIT, *The Wonderful Garden*

"I do, I'm afraid, understand books far more readily than I understand people. Books are so easy to get along with."
—KATHERINE RUNDELL, *Rooftoppers*

Libraries. How I love them. My source of stories. And solitude.
—MITALI PERKINS, *You Bring the Distant Near*

Books are keys that unlock the wisdom of yesterday and open the door to tomorrow.
—SONIA SOTOMAYOR, *Turning Pages*

We all sew a few sequins on our stories to
make them shine brighter.

—CHRISTINA HAMMONDS REED, *The Black Kids*

It feels scary to talk, because once the words are out,
you can't put them back in. But if you write words
and they don't come out the way you want them to,
you can erase them and start over.

—VEERA HIRANANDANI, *The Night Diary*

Every real story is a Neverending Story.

—MICHAEL ENDE, *The Neverending Story*

A story is not true just because of its literal veracity.
It is the message, what it teaches, that counts.

—JOSEPH BRUCHAC, *Dragon Castle*

Fairy tales are more than true: not because they tell
us that dragons exist, but because they tell us that
dragons can be beaten.

—NEIL GAIMAN, *Coraline*
(BY WAY OF G. K. CHESTERTON)

"People who won't listen to arguments or facts can
still be changed by stories."

—JOANNA HO, *The Silence that Binds Us*

"Story magic is powerful, powerful enough to change
someone."

—TAE KELLER, *When You Trap a Tiger*

A good story makes a journey go by more quickly.
A really good story makes you forget you are even
on a journey.

—LYNNE RAE PERKINS, *Nuts to You*

"The stories we tell have power, of course. But the
stories that go untold have just as much power."

—SABAA TAHIR, *A Reaper at the Gates*

"Books . . . are easily destroyed. But words will live as
long as people can remember them."

—TAHEREH MAFI, *Unravel Me*

Even the silence
has a story to tell you.
Just listen. Listen.

—JACQUELINE WOODSON, *Brown Girl Dreaming*

Eat, Drink, and Be Merry

※━━━━※

"Making food always brings people together."
    —VEERA HIRANANDANI, *The Night Diary*

∞ ∞ ∞

I know about chocolate ... "This is what laughing tastes like."
    —KATHERINE APPLEGATE, *Home of the Brave*

∞ ∞ ∞

The first bowl of chocolate pudding was too hot, but Goldilocks ate it all anyway because, hey, it's chocolate pudding, right?
    —MO WILLEMS, *Goldilocks and the Three Dinosaurs*

A good thing
about the bakery is—
If you don't see
what you want,
you'll want
what you see.

  —JAMES STEVENSON, "THE BAKERY," IN *Popcorn*

    ∿ ∿ ∿

"Would it offend the villagers?" the Dragon asked
his Mother, "if I ate their daughters?" . . .
"I believe it would," said his Mother, "so don't,"
and the Dragon didn't.

    —RUMER GODDEN, *The Dragon of Og*

    ∿ ∿ ∿

Somebody who eats pancakes and jam can't be so
awfully dangerous. You can talk to him.

    —TOVE JANSSON, *Finn Family Moomintroll*

"Well," said Frances, "there are many different things to eat, and they taste many different ways. But when I have bread and jam I always know what I am getting, and I am always pleased."

—RUSSELL HOBAN, *Bread and Jam for Frances*

∞ ∞ ∞

What I am
Is tired of jam.
"I want spaghetti and meatballs," said Frances.

—RUSSELL HOBAN, *Bread and Jam for Frances*

∞ ∞ ∞

"My favourite food is cake."
"What kind of cake?"
"It doesn't matter. All cake."

—JENNY HAN, *To All the Boys I've Loved Before*

∞ ∞ ∞

"If more of us valued food and cheer and song above hoarded gold, it would be a merrier world."

—J. R. R. TOLKIEN, *The Hobbit*

"Foods is good and evil, just like people, or badgers, or even scowlers."

"Evil food?" said Charles.

"Parsnips," said Tummeler. "Them's as evil as they come."

—JAMES A. OWEN, *Here, There Be Dragons*

⚭ ⚭ ⚭

We had been eating little bits of things, cake and mince pies, all day, but although they were delicious I was longing for butter and toast, or potatoes with a thick stew. I wanted the certainty of a proper meal, proof that ordinary life was carrying on outside our strange little bubble.

—ROBIN STEVENS, *Mistletoe and Murder*

⚭ ⚭ ⚭

"The worst part of every meal is when it ends."

—V. E. SCHWAB, *The Invisible Life of Addie LaRue*

Indulgence

On Saturday he ate through one piece of chocolate cake, one ice-cream cone, one pickle, one slice of Swiss cheese, one slice of salami, one lollipop, one piece of cherry pie, one sausage, one cupcake, and one slice of watermelon.

That night he had a stomachache!

—ERIC CARLE, *The Very Hungry Caterpillar*

"You can't ever be really free if you admire somebody too much."

—TOVE JANSSON, *Tales from Moominvalley*

Tantrums are seldom about the thing they appear to be about.

—DIANA WYNNE JONES, *Howl's Moving Castle*

♭

"Welcome to America! Where everyone walks around in gym clothes and nobody goes to the gym!"

—KELLY YANG, *Parachutes*

♭

"Why do tycoons with several millions of dollars try to make a billion, a sum so huge they couldn't possibly spend it in a lifetime?"

—WILLIAM PÈNE DU BOIS, *The Twenty-One Balloons*

♭

"You can have it all, but you can't have it all at once."

—REBECCA STEAD, *Goodbye Stranger*

"It's hard to know that you're flying too high until the feathers start dropping."
—DARCIE LITTLE BADGER, *Elatsoe*

♭

"You know, some religious scholars believe that when faced with overwhelming temptation . . . you should commit a small sin, just to relieve the pressure a bit."
—BREE DESPAIN, *The Dark Divine*

"Don't touch things just because they're shiny."
—ZORAIDA CÓRDOVA, *Labyrinth Lost*

♡

"I will do it tomorrow," said Toad. "Today I will take life easy."
—ARNOLD LOBEL, *Days With Frog and Toad*

Adventure and Imagination

"It seems to me," said Edward, "that you won't have had a proper series of adventures unless you've gone through thick and thin."

—AVI, *The End of the Beginning: Being the Adventures of a Small Snail (and an Even Smaller Ant)*

✗ ✗ ✗

"To leave a place, . . . you'd best leave everything behind; all your possessions, including memory. Traveling's not as easy as it's made out to be."

—VIRGINIA HAMILTON, *M.C. Higgins, the Great*

My life is like tofu—it's what gets added that makes it interesting.

—ANGELA JOHNSON, *A Certain October*

✗ ✗ ✗

"You must go on a long journey before you can really find out how wonderful home is."

—TOVE JANSSON, *Comet in Moominland*

✗ ✗ ✗

Grown-up people find it very difficult to believe really wonderful things, unless they have what they call proof.

—E. NESBIT, *Five Children and It*

✗ ✗ ✗

There are things roaming around inside my head as clever as Theseus in the Labyrinth. It's just that nobody ever gave them the necessary piece of string, so they'll never find their way out.

—GERALDINE MCCAUGHREAN, *The White Darkness*

"You haven't been bit till a dragon does it."

—TAMORA PIERCE, *Emperor Mage*

✗ ✗ ✗

Fairy dust is very useful. I use it to turn oatmeal into cake.

—DAVID SHANNON, *Alice the Fairy*

✗ ✗ ✗

"She longed for cutlasses, pistols, and brandy; she had to make do with coffee, and pencils, and verbs."

—PHILIP PULLMAN, *The Tin Princess*

"Imaginary friends are like books. We're created, we're enjoyed, we're dog-eared and creased, and then we're tucked away until we're needed again."

—KATHERINE APPLEGATE, *Crenshaw*

⚸ ⚸ ⚸

There was something wonderful—something potent even—about a present before it's unwrapped. Especially an unexpected one. Anything could be inside.

—KEVIN HENKES, *Junonia*

Sense and Nonsense

"Don't mess with anybody on a Monday. It's a bad, bad day."

—LOUISE FITZHUGH, *Harriet the Spy*

"Know all the Questions, but not the Answers—
Look for the Different, instead of the Same—
Never Walk where there's room for Running—
Don't do anything that can't be a Game."

—ZILPHA KEATLEY SNYDER, *The Changeling*

It is a very funny thing that the sleepier you are,
the longer you take about getting to bed.

—C. S. LEWIS, *The Silver Chair*

"Your trouble comes from years of wearing the wrong kind of shoes."

—ELLEN RASKIN, *The Westing Game*

"Now, remember, Winifred—don't bite your fingernails, don't interrupt when someone else is speaking, and don't go down to the jailhouse at midnight to change places with prisoners."

—NATALIE BABBITT, *Tuck Everlasting*

There is no doubt a new dress is a help under all circumstances.

—NOEL STREATFEILD,
Ballet Shoes

"You shouldn't leave your crayon on other people's beds where it can get sat on."
> —BEVERLY CLEARY, *Ramona the Brave*

"A woman needs a man like a fish needs a bicycle."
I really hate this expression. I bet fish would totally want bicycles, if they had legs.
> —MEG CABOT, *Princess on the Brink*

My mother always said that silence was the best answer to a fool.
> —NNEDI OKORAFOR, *Zahrah the Windseeker*

People nearly always know the right answers, they just like someone else to tell them.
> —CAROLINE RUSH, *Further Tales of Mr. Pengachoosa*

"Beware of gunpowder, and ships' cooks, and pantechnicons, and sausages, and shoes, and ships, and sealing-wax."

—BEATRIX POTTER, *The Tale of Little Pig Robinson*

The trouble with morning is that it comes well before noon.

—LIBBA BRAY, *The Sweet Far Thing*

"Have you noticed how nobody ever looks up? . . . Nobody looks at chimneys, or trees against the sky, or the tops of buildings. Everybody just looks down at the pavement or their shoes. The whole world could pass them by and most people wouldn't notice."

—JULIE ANDREWS EDWARDS,
The Last of the Really Great Whangdoodles

"Whispering makes a narrow place narrower."
> —M. T. ANDERSON, *Feed*

He is everything, everything, everything I ever admired and wanted and couldn't have. He is everything I needed and couldn't find in real life. Of course he is.
That's why I invented him.
> —GERALDINE MCCAUGHREAN, *The White Darkness*

"When something seems like an unbelievable coincidence, then consider that it might not *be* a coincidence."
> —LEILA SALES, *Once Was a Time*

"Even strength has to bow to wisdom sometimes."
—RICK RIORDAN, *Percy Jackson and the Olympians,*
Book One: The Lightning Thief

"Housekeeping ain't no joke."
—LOUISA MAY ALCOTT, *Little Women*

If you had duct tape, you were prepared for anything.
—ANNIE BARROWS, *Ivy + Bean Make the Rules*

Song and Dance

"Not everybody can dance good, but everybody can dance."

—NICOLA YOON, *Instructions for Dancing*

❋ ❋ ❋

"You can live life as a ghost, waiting for death to come, or you can *dance*."

—ALAN GRATZ, *Refugee*

❋ ❋ ❋

How different my life would have been if my parents had just let me dance.

—NNEDI OKORAFOR, *Binti: Home*

"It's dancing! It's magical, actually. A kind of slowish magic. Like writing with your feet."

—KATHERINE RUNDELL, *The Wolf Wilder*

* * *

Music can be more of a home than four walls and a roof.

—SABAA TAHIR, *All My Rage*

* * *

There's always room for a rumba or merengue.

—JUAN FELIPE HERRERA,
Cinnamon Girl: Letters Found Inside a Cereal Box

* * *

So, you never can tell what will happen when you learn to play the harmonica.

—ROBERT MCCLOSKEY, *Lentil*

We all have our la-la-la song. The thing we do when the world isn't singing a nice tune to us. We sing our own nice tune to drown out ugly.

—RITA WILLIAMS-GARCIA, *One Crazy Summer*

✳ ✳ ✳

"We all can dance," he said, "if we find music that we love."

—GILES ANDREAE, *Giraffes Can't Dance*

THREE

How to Be Strong in the World

Life can be difficult. People can disappoint, and not everything can go our way. Children's books remind us that by acknowledging sadness, fear, pain, and setbacks—the hard stuff—we grow stronger; and by sharing our sorrows, we ease them.

Sorrow

Some love is so powerful, after all, that it must always include sadness, because encrypted within it is the knowledge that someday it will come to an end.
  —M. T. ANDERSON, *Symphony for the City of the Dead*

"Grief does not change you, Hazel. It reveals you."
        —JOHN GREEN, *The Fault in Our Stars*

Some wounds go so deep that you don't even feel them until months, maybe years, later.
          —JULIUS LESTER, *When Dad Killed Mom*

"Caring about someone is the best thing there is. We carry the people we miss inside us."
—MARIA PARR, *Adventures with Waffles*

Crying is all right in its way while it lasts. But you have to stop sooner or later and then you still have to decide what to do.
—C. S. LEWIS, *The Silver Chair*

Loss is the wisdom behind song.
—MARILYN NELSON, *Augusta Savage*

Maybe we just lived between hurting and healing.
—BENJAMIN ALIRE SÁENZ,
Aristotle and Dante Discover the Secrets of the Universe

"You gotta face the hand you're dealt and deal with it, and make your problems be the smallest part of who you are."

—JACK GANTOS, *Joey Pigza Swallowed the Key*

The sad truth is that the truth is sad.

—LEMONY SNICKET, *A Series of Unfortunate Events, Book the Ninth: The Carnivorous Carnival*

Life was . . . sad. And yet it was beautiful. The beauty was dimmed when the sadness welled up. And the beauty would be there again when the sadness went. So the beauty and the sadness belonged together somehow, though they were not the same at all.

—WILLIAM STEIG, *Dominic*

For, after all, everyone who wishes to gain
true knowledge must climb the Hill Difficulty
alone, and since there is no royal road to the
summit, I must zigzag it in my own way.

—HELEN KELLER, *The Story of My Life*

"A mistake isn't always a mistake . . . Sometimes a
mistake is actually an opportunity, but we just can't
see it right then and there."

—KELLY YANG, *Front Desk*

"You often learn more by being wrong for the right
reasons than you do by being right for the wrong
reasons."

—NORTON JUSTER, *The Phantom Tollbooth*

"There's no great loss without some small gain."
—LAURA INGALLS WILDER,
Little Town on the Prairie

"Turning an insult into something you embrace is
a good way of empowering yourself."
—CELIA C. PÉREZ, *The First Rule of Punk*

"I mean, there's heartbroken and then there's all the
stuff that comes each second after that, depending on
who broke your heart."
—MARIKO TAMAKI AND JILLIAN TAMAKI, *Skim*

"Can't undo wrong. Can only do our best to make
things right."
—JEWELL PARKER RHODES, *Ghost Boys*

Fear

❖

To fear is one thing. To let fear grab you by
the tail and swing you around is another.
　　　—KATHERINE PATERSON, *Jacob Have I Loved*

"People always fear what they don't understand and destroy what they fear."

—BEN MIKAELSEN, *Ghost of Spirit Bear*

❧

"There are more valuable things in life than safety and comfort."

—NNEDI OKORAFOR, *Akata Witch*

❧

"If you put things off for later, you'll never do them. They'll become harder and scarier, and one day you'll realize you've run out of time."

—TAE KELLER, *When You Trap a Tiger*

❧

Funny how sometimes you worry a lot about something and it turns out to be nothing.

—R. J. PALACIO, *Wonder*

It is one thing to say that something should be done, but quite a different matter to do it.

—AESOP, "BELLING THE CAT," IN
The Aesop for Children

Doing something that scares one a little, each and every day, helps one grow as a person.

—SALLY J. PLA, *The Someday Birds*

Scary with you is better than scary without you.

—TAMORA PIERCE, *Emperor Mage*

Piglet was so excited at the idea of being Useful that he forgot to be frightened any more.

—A. A. MILNE, *Winnie-the-Pooh*

Defiance

"It *is* helpful to know the proper way to behave, so one can decide whether or not to be proper."
—GAIL CARSON LEVINE, *Ella Enchanted*

There are some people who just make you want to see how far you can go.
—JUDY BLUME, *Blubber*

"Stay angry, little Meg," Mrs. Whatsit whispered. "You will need all your anger now."
—MADELEINE L'ENGLE, *A Wrinkle in Time*

"You must admit I have a right to live in a pigsty if I want."

—DIANA WYNNE JONES, *Howl's Moving Castle*

Wise as she was, she realized that people can postpone their rebellious phases until they're eighty-five years old, and she decided to keep an eye on herself.

—TOVE JANSSON, *The Summer Book*

Neatness was not one of the things he aimed at in life.

—GEORGE SELDEN, *The Cricket in Times Square*

If you ever find yourself in the wrong story, leave.
—MO WILLEMS, *Goldilocks and the Three Dinosaurs*

"Truth is dangerous. It topples palaces and kills kings. It stirs gentle men to rage and bids them take up arms. It wakes old grievances and opens forgotten wounds. It is the mother of the sleepless night and the hag-ridden day. And yet there is one thing that is more dangerous than Truth. Those who would silence Truth's voice are more destructive by far."
—FRANCES HARDINGE, *Fly by Night*

Without a doubt, there is such a thing as too much order.
—ARNOLD LOBEL,
"THE CROCODILE IN THE BEDROOM," IN *Fables*

"Doors are for people with no imagination."
—DEREK LANDY, *Skulduggery Pleasant*

What I'm finding out about growing older is that there are just as many rules about lots of things, but there's nobody watching.
—PHYLLIS REYNOLDS NAYLOR,
Alice in Rapture, Sort Of

One can never consent to creep when one feels an impulse to soar.
—HELEN KELLER, *The Story of My Life*

"There are people who will try to make you choose between who you are and who they want you to be. You have to watch out for those people."
—REBECCA STEAD,
The List of Things That Will Not Change

People Are Complicated

Observable Fact: People aren't logical.

   —NICOLA YOON, *The Sun Is Also a Star*

Any rat in a sewer can lie. It's how rats are. It's what makes them rats. But a human doesn't run and hide in dark places, because he's something more. Lying is the most personal act of cowardice there is.

"I'm really a very good man; but I'm a very bad Wizard."

   —L. FRANK BAUM, *The Wonderful Wizard of Oz*

"Any rat in a sewer can lie. It's how rats are. It's what makes them rats. But a human doesn't run and hide in dark places, because he's something more. Lying is the most personal act of cowardice there is."

   —NANCY FARMER, *The House of the Scorpion*

"What you *can* do is often simply a matter of what you *will* do."

—NORTON JUSTER, *The Phantom Tollbooth*

∞ ∞ ∞

"Never dismiss anyone's value until you know him."

—SUSAN COOPER, *Greenwitch*

∞ ∞ ∞

I think sometimes that people are like
onions. On the outside smooth and whole
and simple but inside ring upon ring, complex
and deep.

—KAREN CUSHMAN, *Catherine, Called Birdy*

"A clown needn't be the same out of the ring as he has to be when he's in it. If you look at photographs of clowns when they're just being ordinary men, they've got quite sad faces."

—ENID BLYTON, *Five Go off in a Caravan*

∞ ∞ ∞

There is not always a good guy. Nor is there always a bad one. Most people are somewhere in between.

—PATRICK NESS, *A Monster Calls*

∞ ∞ ∞

"It is most perilous to be a speaker of Truth. Sometimes one must choose to be silent, or be silenced. But if a truth cannot be spoken, it must at least be known. Even if you dare not speak truth to others, never lie to yourself."

—FRANCES HARDINGE, *Fly by Night*

"People aren't either wicked or noble . . .
They're like chef's salads, with good things
and bad things chopped and mixed together
in a vinaigrette of confusion and conflict."
  —LEMONY SNICKET, *A Series of Unfortunate Events,
Book the Eleventh: The Grim Grotto*

∞ ∞ ∞

"I like flaws, I think they make things interesting."
  —SARAH DESSEN, *The Truth about Forever*

∞ ∞ ∞

"You can't always judge people by the things they
done. You got to judge them by what they are doing
now."
  —KATE DICAMILLO, *Because of Winn-Dixie*

∞ ∞ ∞

"If you are strong, you can hold more than one truth
in your heart."
  —TAE KELLER, *When You Trap a Tiger*

Individuality

Our differences are our *superpowers*.

—CECE BELL, *El Deafo*

♥

What you see and hear depends a good deal on where you are standing: it also depends on what sort of person you are.

—C. S. LEWIS, *The Magician's Nephew*

♥

"You ever consider that maybe you not supposed to 'fit'? People who make history rarely do."

—NIC STONE, *Dear Martin*

Everyone is smart in different ways. But if you judge a fish on its ability to climb a tree, it will spend its whole life thinking that it's stupid.

—LYNDA MULLALY HUNT, *Fish in a Tree*

"The thing about chameleoning your way through life is that it gets to where nothing is real."

—JOHN GREEN, *An Abundance of Katherines*

Maybe I'm not so different from everyone else after all. It's like somebody gave me a puzzle, but I don't have the box with the picture on it. So I don't know what the final thing is supposed to look like. I'm not even sure if I have all the pieces.

—SHARON M. DRAPER, *Out of My Mind*

"Ninety percent of who you are is invisible."
—E. L. KONIGSBERG,
The Mysterious Edge of the Heroic World

There will be times when you walk into a room
and no one there is quite like you until the day
you begin

to share your stories . . .

And all at once, in the room where no one else is
quite like you,
the world opens itself up a little wider
to make some space for you.
—JACQUELINE WOODSON, *The Day You Begin*

We prefer to explore the universe by traveling inward,
as opposed to outward.
—NNEDI OKORAFOR, *Binti*

"It's important to know what you think, my dear, or else you will be so hemmed in by other people's ideas and opinions, you won't have room for your own."

—KAREN CUSHMAN,
The Loud Silence of Francine Green

"I promise you I will never again try to turn myself into a stylish dandy," said Dandelion as he sipped his tea. "From now on I'll always be just plain me!"

—DON FREEMAN, *Dandelion*

FOUR

How to Be at Home
in the World

❯───────❯───────❮

Find your people. Appreciate animals. Respect the earth. Leave things a little better than you found them. Children's books help us understand that we belong, and belonging includes caring for loved ones and cherishing nature and all living things.

Family

"There is no place like home."
—L. FRANK BAUM, *The Wonderful Wizard of Oz*

"This is how you hold on to your family . . . You hold them with open hands so they are free to find futures of their own."
—RICHARD PECK, *Secrets at Sea*

Mothers are the parachutes.
—JANDY NELSON, *I'll Give You the Sun*

I think all of us are always five years old in the presence and absence of our parents.

—SHERMAN ALEXIE,
The Absolutely True Diary of a Part-Time Indian

"No family is perfect. Get that idea out of your head. And nobody is perfect either. All we can do is work at it. And we do."

—BEVERLY CLEARY, *Ramona and Her Father*

I can't make my brothers
go live elsewhere,
but I can
hide their sandals.

—THANHHA LAI, *Inside Out and Back Again*

"But we're never what our parents expected.
They have to learn that lesson."
—MALINDA LO, *Last Night at the Telegraph Club*

✗ ✗ ✗

But now that her moms were listening, now that they
were trying to understand, Joey could close her eyes,
enjoy the feeling of their arms wrapped around her,
and feel hopeful.
—NICOLE MELLEBY, *The Science of Being Angry*

✗ ✗ ✗

Nobody in my family is fancy at all. They never even
ask for sprinkles.
—JANE O'CONNOR, *Fancy Nancy*

✗ ✗ ✗

Sometimes the apple rolls very far from the tree.
—SARA PENNYPACKER, *Pax*

Sometimes even mamas make mistakes.
—JUDITH VIORST, *My Mama Says There Aren't
Any Zombies, Ghosts, Vampires, Creatures,
Demons, Monsters, Fiends, Goblins, or Things*

Human babies are only tiny for an instant—their
growing up is as swift as the beat of a hummingbird's
wing.
—KELLY BARNHILL, *The Girl Who Drank the Moon*

Home is the people I surround myself with, the ones
I break bread with. The keepers of my secrets and
my fears. It is to be loved and to give love without
inhibitions.
—LILLIAM RIVERA, *Dealing in Dreams*

Friendship

It's not often that someone comes along who is a true friend and good writer. Charlotte was both.
——E. B. WHITE, *Charlotte's Web*

"But you can't give up on people. It's one of the three keys of friendship. You gotta listen, you gotta care, and most importantly, you gotta keep trying."
——KELLY YANG, *Three Keys*

"Friends should always tell each other the truth."
——JAMES MARSHALL, "SPLIT PEA SOUP," IN
*George and Martha: The Complete Stories
of Two Best Friends*

One of the hazards of having friends, especially longtime ones, is just how well they know you.
—NICOLA YOON, *Instructions for Dancing*

Talk was like the vitamins of our friendship: Large daily doses kept it healthy.
—E. L. KONIGSBERG, *Silent to the Bone*

Even angry words were better than silence.
—NANCY FARMER, *The House of the Scorpion*

"I don't need a bunch of fake friends. I only need one. One real friend."
—ALICIA WILLIAMS, *Genesis Begins Again*

We may not like it, but we need human friends, because we have human enemies whether we will or nay.

— ROBIN MCKINLEY, *Spindle's End*

"The bravest person I know is afraid of the dark. She sleeps with a night lamp always, but if her friends are threatened? She suddenly thinks she's a bear twelve feet tall and attacks whoever scared her friends."

— TAMORA PIERCE, *Cold Fire*

Friends are always worth the moments of joy you share, even if they don't last.

— ERIC GANSWORTH, *If I Ever Get Out of Here*

"I think everyone in the world is friends, if you can only get them to see you don't want to be un-friends."

— E. NESBIT, *The Railway Children*

It is so good to have friends who understand how there is a time for crying and a time for laughing, and that sometimes the two are very close together.

—LOIS LOWRY, *A Summer to Die*

A circle's round, it has no end,
That's how long I will be your friend.
—CHRISTINA HAMMONDS REED, *The Black Kids*

Community

Trouble can always be borne when it is shared.
—KATHERINE PATERSON,
The Tale of the Mandarin Ducks

❊ ❊ ❊

Different languages, different food, different customs. That's our neighborhood: wild and tangled and colorful. Like the best kind of garden.
—KATHERINE APPLEGATE, *Wishtree*

❊ ❊ ❊

"If we truly trust no one, we cannot survive."
—MEGAN WHALEN TURNER, *The King of Attolia*

we'd been trying to touch the sky from the bottom of the ocean. I realized that if we boosted one another, maybe we'd get a little closer.

—RUTA SEPETYS, *Between Shades of Gray*

❋ ❋ ❋

"Whether someone is useful only matters if you value people by their use."

—CORINNE DUYVIS, *On the Edge of Gone*

❋ ❋ ❋

Anybody who thinks small towns are friendlier than big cities lives in a big city.

—RICHARD PECK, *A Year Down Yonder*

❋ ❋ ❋

"You don't have to like everyone, but you don't have to be a jerk about it, either!"

—JERRY CRAFT, *New Kid*

"We should always have some aim in life which we must try to achieve while being of help to others."
　　　　—SUDHA MURTY, *Grandma's Bag of Stories*

❋ ❋ ❋

"People's souls are like gardens . . . You can't turn your back on someone because his garden's full of weeds. You have to give him water and lots of sunlight."
　　　　—NANCY FARMER, *The House of the Scorpion*

❋ ❋ ❋

"Them as can do, has to do for them as can't. And someone has to speak up for them as has no voices."
　　　　—TERRY PRATCHETT, *The Wee Free Men*

❋ ❋ ❋

There's as many ways to live as people.
　　　　—LOUISE FITZHUGH, *Harriet the Spy*

You sometimes don't know you exist until you realize someone like you existed before.

— GEORGE M. JOHNSON, *All Boys Aren't Blue*

❀ ❀ ❀

Faith had always told herself that she was not like other ladies. But neither, it seemed, were other ladies.

— FRANCES HARDINGE, *The Lie Tree*

❀ ❀ ❀

"Every stone is different. No other stone exactly like it . . . God loves variety . . . In odd days like these . . . people study how to be all alike instead of how to be as different as they really are."

— MONICA SHANNON, *Dobry*

❀ ❀ ❀

"The highest law for us is to live for one another."

— VIRGINIA HAMILTON, *The Planet of Junior Brown*

Animals

"Whatever you do to the animals, you do to yourself."

—BEN MIKAELSEN, *Touching Spirit Bear*

Is there anything sweeter than the touch of another as she pulls a dead bug from your fur?

—KATHERINE APPLEGATE, *The One and Only Ivan*

"It is a much more straightforward thing to be a dog, and a dog's love, once given, is not reconsidered."

—ROBIN MCKINLEY, *Deerskin*

He could tell by the way the animals walked that
they were keeping time to some kind of music.
Maybe it was the song in their own hearts that
they walked to.

   —LAURA ADAMS ARMER, *Waterless Mountain*

"Sometimes a person really must
choose between two good things."
Two good things, thought Flora.
"I would choose the thing that involved a cat,"
she said.

     —CYNTHIA RYLANT, *Rosetown Summer*

You don't need tickets
To listen to crickets.

—DOUGLAS FLORIAN,
"THE CRICKETS," IN *Insectlopedia*

Many dogs can understand almost every word
humans say, while humans seldom learn to recognize
more than half a dozen barks, if that.
  —DODIE SMITH, *The Hundred and One Dalmatians*

"If we'd been edible, we'd never have lasted this long."

—RUSSELL HOBAN, *The Mouse and His Child*

If a lion comes to visit
Don't open your door
Just firmly ask "What is it?"
And listen to him roar.

—KARLA KUSKIN, *Roar and More*

The rattlesnake would be a lot more dangerous if it didn't have a rattle.

—LOUIS SACHAR, *Holes*

Dolphin, it was from your marine caress
That I learned gentleness.

—VIKRAM SETH, *Arion and the Dolphin*

A lion in a zoo,
Shut up in a cage,
Lives a life
Of smothered rage.

—LANGSTON HUGHES, "A LION IN A ZOO," IN
The Sweet and Sour Animal Book

"I think the smell of horses is the most exciting smell
in the world."

—ZILPHA KEATLEY SNYDER, *The Changeling*

Nature

⟩————⟨

I will treat . . .
the winged ones,
the crawling ones,
the four-legged,
the two-legged,
the plants,
trees,
rivers,
lakes,
the Earth
with kindness and respect.

—CAROLE LINDSTROM, "EARTH STEWARD
AND WATER PROTECTOR PLEDGE," IN
We Are Water Protectors

"No matter how old a person gets, he's never old in spring!"

—ELIZABETH ENRIGHT, *Return to Gone-Away*

Man might carve his mark on the earth, but unless he's vigilant, Nature will take it all back.

—WITI IHIMAERA, *The Whale Rider*

"You must have a garden. Wherever you are."

—PATRICIA MACLACHLAN, *Sarah, Plain and Tall*

My sister had taught me to look at the world that way, as a place that glitters, as a place where the calls of the crickets and the crows and the wind are everyday occurrences that also happen to be magic.

—CYNTHIA KADOHATA, *Kira-Kira*

∽➿∾

"If you spend enough time in the desert, you will hear it speak."

—NNEDI OKORAFOR, *Who Fears Death*

∽➿∾

"The human body is ten percent hydrogen. Which means ten percent of us is as old as the universe itself."

—TAE KELLER, *Jennifer Chan Is Not Alone*

∽➿∾

I bet you could sometimes find all the mysteries of the universe in someone's hand.

—BENJAMIN ALIRE SÁENZ,
Aristotle and Dante Discover the Secrets of the Universe

"What makes the desert beautiful," the little prince said, "is that it hides a well somewhere . . ."
　　—ANTOINE DE SAINT-EXUPÉRY, *The Little Prince*

∽∾∽

"I like it better here where I can sit just quietly and smell the flowers."
　　—MUNRO LEAF, *The Story of Ferdinand*

FIVE

How to Believe in the World

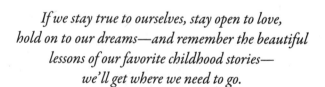

*If we stay true to ourselves, stay open to love,
hold on to our dreams—and remember the beautiful
lessons of our favorite childhood stories—
we'll get where we need to go.*

Optimism

A seed is a promise . . . a guarantee. Plant it and watch it grow.

—TRACEY BAPTISTE, *The Jumbies*

"These are hard times. The world hurts. We live in fear and forget to walk with hope. But hope has not forgotten you. So ask it to dinner. It's probably hungry and would appreciate the invitation."

—LIBBA BRAY, *Going Bovine*

"Tomorrow is a new day with no mistakes in it yet."

—L. M. MONTGOMERY, *Anne of Green Gables*

"Impossible?" the goldfish man said. "Don't you see? Even fates written in the Book of Fortune can be changed. How can anything be impossible?"
    —GRACE LIN, *Where the Mountain Meets the Moon*

A good day wasn't a day without clouds but rather a day when one focused on finding the sunlight behind the clouds.
    —BEN MIKAELSEN, *Ghost of Spirit Bear*

And everyone lived happily, though maybe not completely honestly, ever after. *The End.*
    —JON SCIESZKA,
    The Stinky Cheese Man and Other Fairly Stupid Tales

"Cynics are people who are afraid to believe."
—KATE DICAMILLO,
Flora and Ulysses: The Illuminated Adventures

"Today was a difficult day. Tomorrow will be better."
—KEVIN HENKES, *Lilly's Purple Plastic Purse*

"Sometimes when you're surrounded by dirt . . .
you're a better witness for what's beautiful."
—MATT DE LA PEÑA, *Last Stop on Market Street*

Love

⟡———⟡

"What is given from the heart reaches the heart."
—PATRICIA MCKISSACK,
What Is Given from the Heart

∞ ∞ ∞

Maybe when my mother claimed there was no word for love, she was really saying that no word could encompass all the different ways we find it.
—ERIC GANSWORTH, *Apple: Skin to the Core*

∞ ∞ ∞

Just because she's dead it doesn't mean I stopped loving her or that she stopped loving me. It's just her body that left. The love didn't.
—JULIUS LESTER, *When Dad Killed Mom*

"Love isn't like a cup of sugar that gets used up."
—BEVERLY CLEARY, *Ramona the Brave*

∞ ∞ ∞

Nothing is sweeter in this sad world than the sound of someone you love calling your name.
—KATE DICAMILLO, *The Tale of Despereaux*

∞ ∞ ∞

Do not forget about the thorns on the roses when you say love is like a red red rose.
—ISABEL QUINTERO, *Gabi, a Girl in Pieces*

"A person doesn't have to be here to love you."
        —MORRIS GLEITZMAN, *Then*

∞ ∞ ∞

Love is about the good moments, but it's about holding on to each other during the difficult ones too.
        —AISHA SAEED, *Written in the Stars*

∞ ∞ ∞

"Well, it's simple to love someone," she said. "But it's hard to know when you need to say it out loud."
        —REBECCA STEAD, *When You Reach Me*

∞ ∞ ∞

Maybe that was how it was with all first loves. They own a little piece of your heart, always.
        —JENNY HAN, *We'll Always Have Summer*

"It's okay to keep something you love just for you."
— ADIB KHORRAM, *Darius the Great Deserves Better*

∞ ∞ ∞

"At an early age I learned that people make mistakes, and you have to decide if their mistakes are bigger than your love for them."
— ANGIE THOMAS, *The Hate U Give*

∞ ∞ ∞

He was happy and unhappy all at once. He was in love.
— PETRA MATHERS, *Victor and Christabel*

∞ ∞ ∞

I would hold her hand forever if I could.
But I can't. So I let go.
I love her, and I have to let go.
— SARA FARIZAN, *If You Could Be Mine*

Perseverance

"The first hole's the hardest."
—LOUIS SACHAR, *Holes*

♥

I think I can. I think I can. I think I can.
—WATTY PIPER, *The Little Engine That Could*

♥

"Remember how with patience and calm, even a donkey can climb a palm tree!"
—JULIA ALVAREZ, *How Tía Lola Saved the Summer*

"When every door is closed, one
learns to climb through windows."
—FRANCES HARDINGE, *The Lie Tree*

❦

"Good things come, but they're never perfect;
are they? You have to twist them into something
perfect."
—MAUD HART LOVELACE, *Betsy's Wedding*

❦

"Things come at you—balls, clubs,
knives, sorrow, loss. Either you
stand there and let them hit you
or you throw them back *pugnis
et calcibus*, with all your might."
—KAREN CUSHMAN,
Will Sparrow's Road

"And if my choice is to sit graciously in my best robes and accept the inevitable or to bail a sea with a bucket, give me the bucket."
—ROBIN MCKINLEY, *Chalice*

❥

One step at a time . . . one day at a time. Just today— just this day to get through . . .
—LINDA SUE PARK, *A Long Walk to Water*

❥

"You cannot keep your eyes on the bloody footprints you have left behind you. You must keep your eyes on where you are going."
—TIM TINGLE, *How I Became a Ghost*

❥

Sometimes the only thing to say about a period of time is that it's passing and that you're surviving it.
—NICOLA YOON, *Instructions for Dancing*

And I realize that the decision to be human is not one single instant, but is a thousand choices made every day. It is choices we make every second and requires constant vigilance. We have to fight to remain human.

—M. T. ANDERSON, *Thirsty*

"Do not ever be afraid to start over."

—PAM MUÑOZ RYAN, *Esperanza Rising*

Becoming Who You're Meant to Be

◆━━━◆

"I took a lot of wrong turns to find out who I really was. You will, too."

— SHARON FLAKE, *The Skin I'm In*

✕ ✕ ✕

"Dad says I'm a late bloomer."
"Maybe. Or maybe you're blooming now, and you're just not the kind of flower he was expecting."

— ALEX GINO, *Rick*

✕ ✕ ✕

I only know that learning to believe in the power of my own words has been the most freeing experience of my life. It has brought me the most light.

— ELIZABETH ACEVEDO, *The Poet X*

I'm not sure which matters more—where the seed comes from, or where it takes root and grows.
     —ZETTA ELLIOTT, *A Wish After Midnight*

❌ ❌ ❌

A name is important. It isn't something you drop in the litter basket or on the ground. Your name is how people know you.
     —RITA WILLIAMS-GARCIA, *One Crazy Summer*

❌ ❌ ❌

If it means anything at all to live in this world, it's that you must live your life like a true human being and feel just what you feel.
     —GENZABURŌ YOSHINO, *How Do You Live?*

❌ ❌ ❌

"I think you gotta be who you want to be until you feel like you are whoever it is you're trying to become. Sometimes half of doing something is pretending that you can."
     —JULIE MURPHY, *Dumplin'*

"Because I am exactly where I should be, doing exactly what I should be doing. That is peace."

—SARA PENNYPACKER, *Pax*

✗ ✗ ✗

"Own your power, own your connection to Mother Earth. Howl at the moon, bare your teeth, and be a goddamn wolf."

—GABBY RIVERA, *Juliet Takes a Breath*

✗ ✗ ✗

It's like I've spent my whole life fiddling with a complicated combination only to discover I was toying with the wrong lock.

—JASMINE WARGA, *My Heart and Other Black Holes*

✗ ✗ ✗

"I guess sometimes you don't know what you want because you don't know it exists."

—LYNDA MULLALY HUNT, *One for the Murphys*

I was born royalty. All I had to do was pick up my crown.

—LEAH JOHNSON, *You Should See Me in a Crown*

Choices

"You can't run away from who you are, but what you can do is run toward who you want to be."

—JASON REYNOLDS, *Ghost*

Settle for what you can get, but first ask for the World.

—DIANA WYNNE JONES,
The Tough Guide to Fantasyland

I am anything I wish to be. The world cannot choose for me. No, it is for me to choose what the world shall be.
—FRANCES HARDINGE, *The Lost Conspiracy*

"You can't be the rock and the river, Sam . . .
The rock is high ground . . . Solid. Immovable . . .
The river is motion, turmoil, rage.
"As the river flows, it wonders what it would be like
to be so still, to take a breath, to rest. But the rock
will always wonder what lies around the bend
in the stream."
"I want to be both," I whispered.

— KEKLA MAGOON, *The Rock and the River*

"You have to fight to take back control of your life.
Sometimes you will hurt the ones you love the most.
But in the end, it will always have to be your choice."

— SABINA KHAN, *The Love and Lies of Rukhsana Ali*

"You're either a doer, or a spectator. And the world
already got enough spectators."

— B. B. ALSTON, "THE MCCOY GAME," IN *Black Boy Joy*

"You mean you're comparing our lives to a sonnet?
A strict form, but freedom within it?"
"Yes," Mrs. Whatsit said. "You're given the form,
but you have to write the sonnet yourself."
—MADELEINE L'ENGLE, *A Wrinkle in Time*

"Baby, we have no choice of what color we're born or
who our parents are or whether we're rich or poor.
What we do have is some choice over what we make
of our lives once we're here."
—MILDRED D. TAYLOR,
Roll of Thunder, Hear My Cry

"The best way to treat obstacles is to use them as
stepping-stones. Laugh at them, tread on them, and
let them lead you to something better."
—ENID BLYTON, *Mr. Galliano's Circus*

I envy the trees
that grow
at crossroads.
They are never
forced
to decide
which way
to go . . .
—MARGARITA ENGLE,
The Lightning Dreamer

"I wish it need not have happened in
my time," said Frodo.
"So do I," said Gandalf, "and so do all who
live to see such times. But that is not for
them to decide. All we have to decide is what
to do with the time that is given us."
—J. R. R. TOLKIEN,
The Fellowship of the Ring

"To say you have no choice is to release yourself from responsibility."

——PATRICK NESS, *Monsters of Men*

Some people could hold on to many different dreams and see them all come true.

——AISHA SAEED, *Amal Unbound*

Since then I had learned the most important thing: the decisions you make can become your life. Your choices are you.

——DAVID BARCLAY MOORE,
The Stars Beneath Our Feet

Change

Does a metamorphosis begin
from the outside in?
Or from the inside out?

—PAM MUÑOZ RYAN, *The Dreamer*

❋ ❋ ❋

"Change takes time. And patience. And . . .
a willingness to listen to people we may not
understand."

—BRANDY COLBERT, *The Voting Booth*

❋ ❋ ❋

What's the point of having a voice if you're gonna be
silent in those moments you shouldn't be?

—ANGIE THOMAS, *The Hate U Give*

I'd seen myself as broken. But couldn't you be broken and still bring change?
—NNEDI OKORAFOR, *Binti: The Night Masquerade*

❋ ❋ ❋

"Minds, like diapers, need occasional changing."
—KAREN CUSHMAN, *The Ballad of Lucy Whipple*

❋ ❋ ❋

"It's no use going back to yesterday, because I was a different person *then*."
—LEWIS CARROLL, *Alice's Adventures in Wonderland and Through the Looking-Glass*

❋ ❋ ❋

"Nothing is lost . . . Everything is transformed."
—MICHAEL ENDE, *The Neverending Story*

Everything changes, for better or worse, whether we like it or not. Sometimes it's beautiful, and sometimes it fills us with terror. Sometimes both.

—ERIKA L. SÁNCHEZ,
I Am Not Your Perfect Mexican Daughter

❄ ❄ ❄

"If you don't see anything beautiful, change your viewpoint."

—ERIN ENTRADA KELLY, *You Go First*

❄ ❄ ❄

"You can't change the past, but you can do better in the future."

—KWAME ALEXANDER, *An American Story*

❄ ❄ ❄

"Sometimes, if you want to change a man's mind, you change the mind of the man next to him first."

—MEGAN WHALEN TURNER, *The King of Attolia*

"The future cannot blame the present, just as the present cannot blame the past. The hope is always here, always alive, but only your fierce caring can fan it into a fire to warm the world."

—SUSAN COOPER, *Silver on the Tree*

＊ ＊ ＊

"Today we're going to be like the earth, spinning around and affecting many. Today we're going to think about our part in the revolution."

—RITA WILLIAMS-GARCIA, *One Crazy Summer*

＊ ＊ ＊

Someday we will become something we haven't even yet imagined.

—YUYI MORALES, *Dreamers*

Faith, Hope, and Possibility

"Belief in mysteries—all manner of mysteries—is the only lasting luxury in life."
—ZILPHA KEATLEY SNYDER, *The Witches of Worm*

Because we have a right, my grandfather tells us . . .
to walk and sit and dream wherever we want.
—JACQUELINE WOODSON, *Brown Girl Dreaming*

Why are people afraid to believe? Maybe it's because if they believe in a better world, then they have to work to make that world happen.
—TAE KELLER, *Jennifer Chan Is Not Alone*

I want to say, before anything, that dreams are very important.

—MAIRA KALMAN, *Max Makes a Million*

The bell still rings for me as it does for all who truly believe.

—CHRIS VAN ALLSBURG, *The Polar Express*

"Every man has a last choice after the first, a chance of forgiveness. It is not too late. Turn. Come to the Light."

—SUSAN COOPER, *The Dark Is Rising*

Dreams don't have timelines,
deadlines,
and aren't always in
straight lines.

—JASON REYNOLDS, *For Every One*

"The most important part of religion isn't in any church. It's down in your own heart. Religion is in your thoughts, and in the way you act from day to day, in the way you treat other people. It's honesty, and unselfishness, and kindness. Especially kindness."

—MAUD HART LOVELACE, *Heaven to Betsy*

"But dying's part of the wheel, right there next to being born. You can't pick out the pieces you like and leave the rest. Being part of the whole thing, that's the blessing."

—NATALIE BABBITT, *Tuck Everlasting*

Don't ever stop dreaming big
But for now, put that dream on paper
It's easier to carry around
  —IBI ZOBOI AND YUSEF SALAAM, *Punching the Air*

Anyone can fly. All you need is somewhere to go that you can't get to any other way. The next thing you know, you're flying among the stars.

—FAITH RINGGOLD, *Tar Beach*

"I do not need a marker of my passage, for my creator knows where I am. I do not want anyone to cry. I lived a good life, my hair turned to snow, I saw my great-grandchildren, I grew my garden. That is all."

—LOUISE ERDRICH, *Makoons*

I don't know what is going to happen next year, no one does. But that's OK.
I can handle it, I decide. It's just a harder gear, and I am ready. All I have to do is take a deep breath and ride.

—MEG MEDINA, *Merci Suárez Changes Gears*

What you believe about the future will change how you live in the present.

—DANIEL NAYERI, *Everything Sad Is Untrue*

Hold fast to dreams
For if dreams die
Life is a broken-winged bird
That cannot fly.

—LANGSTON HUGHES, "DREAMS,"
IN *The Dream Keeper and Other Poems*

"Just because you don't see the path doesn't mean it's not there."

—VARIAN JOHNSON, *The Parker Inheritance*

"It may not be your dream, Stepsister, but do not scoff at those who do dream of it."

—MALINDA LO, Ash

The beauty of the world is an everyday gift. All you need . . . is to reach out and receive it.

—JULIA ALVAREZ, *How Tía Lola Came to ~~Visit~~ Stay*

ACKNOWLEDGMENTS

THANKS FIRST TO THE WRITERS AND artists who invited us into the world of books and reading when we were children, and who fired our imaginations, strengthened our empathy, and enriched our knowledge of our world, near and far. Thanks to our children, Nick Becker and Tristan Chapman, who pulled us joyfully back into the evolving and yet eternally wise world of children's books when we became parents. We're grateful to Olive Fretts Howard, Alex Valenti, and Margaret Bauer, all of whom helped us wrangle our work and check these quotations. We're lucky to have been able to work with everyone at Algonquin Books, especially our copyeditor, Sue Wilkins, along with Brunson Hoole, Marisol Salaman, Debra Linn, Christopher Moisan, Michael McKenzie, Jovanna Brinck, Julia Primavera, Steve Godwin, and our phenomenal editor, Betsy Gleick, who knew the time was right for this book and made it happen. Thanks to R. J. Palacio for a perfect foreword and to Eleanor Davis for her delightful illustrations. Thanks to Diane Kraut for handling permissions and to Tom Brooke for his wise counsel. We're so glad for the ways Jordan Laney and Jed Fretts Howard enrich our lives. To our partners, Leo Chapman and Stephen Churchville, who have inspired us and sustained us every day—gratitude and love.

PERMISSIONS

INDEX OF BOOKS AND AUTHORS

◆────────────◆

Absolutely True Diary of a Part-Time Indian, The, 86

Abundance of Katherines, An, 79

Acevedo, Elizabeth, 18, 120

Achingly Alice, 8

Adeyemi, Tomi, 13

Adventures of Pinocchio, The, 7

Adventures with Waffles, 62

Aesop, 69

Aesop for Children, The: "Belling the Cat," 69

Akata Witch, 68

Alcott, Louisa May, 20, 54

Alexander and the Terrible, Horrible, No Good, Very Bad Day, 11

Alexander, Kwame, 18, 131

Alexie, Sherman, 86

Alice in Rapture, Sort Of, 73

Alice the Fairy, 47

Alice's Adventures in Wonderland and Through the Looking-Glass, 130

All Boys Aren't Blue: A Memoir-Manifesto, 97

All My Rage, 56

All the Bright Places, 7

Alston, B. B., 125

Alvarez, Julia, 116, 139

Amal Unbound, 13, 128

American Story, An, 131

Anderson, Laurie Halse, 14

Anderson, M. T., 6, 53, 61, 119

Andreae, Giles, 57

Anne of Green Gables, 109

Anne of the Island, 22

Apple: Skin to the Core, 112

Applegate, Katherine, 37, 48, 93, 98

Arion and the Dolphin, 101

Aristotle and Dante Discover the Secrets of the Universe, 3, 62, 105

Armer, Laura Adams, 99

Ash, 11, 139

Augusta Savage: The Shape of a Sculptor's Life, 62

Avi, 45

Babbitt, Natalie, 50, 135

Ballad of Lucy Whipple, The, 130

Ballet Shoes, 50

Baptiste, Tracey, 109

Barnhill, Kelly, 4, 88

Barrie, J. M., 6

Barrows, Annie, 54

Baum, L. Frank, 74, 85

Because of Winn-Dixie, 77

Bell, Cece, 78

Betsy's Wedding, 117

Between Shades of Gray, 94

Binti, 80

Binti: Home, 55

Binti: The Night Masquerade, 130

*Black Boy Joy: 17 Stories
    Celebrating Black Boyhood:*
    "The Griot of Grover Street," 28

*Black Boy Joy: 17 Stories
    Celebrating Black Boyhood:*
    "The McCoy Game," 125

Black Kids, The, 34, 92

Blubber, 70

Blume, Judy, 70

Blyton, Enid, 76, 126

Book of Phoenix, The, 32

Boynton, Sandra, 20

Bray, Libba, 23, 52, 109

Bread and Jam for Frances, 39

Brown Girl Dreaming, 36, 133

Bruchac, Joseph, 35

Bud, Not Buddy, 10

Burcaw, Shane, 30

Burnett, Frances Hodgson, 5, 27

Cabot, Meg, 51

Carle, Eric, 41

*Carnivorous Carnival, The
    (A Series of Unfortunate
    Events, Book the Ninth)*, 63

Carroll, Lewis, 130

Castle in the Air, 4

Catherine, Called Birdy, 75

Certain October, A, 46

Chain of Iron, 23

Chains, 14

Chalice, 118

Changeling, The, 49, 102

Charlotte's Web, 89

Children of Blood and Bone, 13

*Cinnamon Girl: Letters Found Inside
    a Cereal Box*, 56

City of Death, 14

Clare, Cassandra, 23

Cleary, Beverly, 8, 22, 51, 86, 113

Colasanti, Susane, 23

Colbert, Brandy, 12, 127

Cold Fire, 91

Collodi, C., 7

Comet in Moominland, 46

Cooper, Susan, 8, 75, 132, 134

Coraline, 35

Córdova, Zoraida, 44

Craft, Jerry, 94

Crenshaw, 48

Cricket in Times Square, The, 71

Crossover, The: "Basketball Rule #3," 18

Curtis, Christopher Paul, 10

Cushman, Karen, 18, 75, 81, 117, 130

Dahl, Roald, 19

Dandelion, 81

Darius the Great Deserves Better, 115

Dark Divine, The, 15, 43

Dark Is Rising, The, 134

Day of Tears, 3

Day You Begin, The, 80

Days With Frog and Toad, 44

de la Peña, Matt, 111

Dealing in Dreams, 88

Dear Martin, 78

Deerskin, 98

Despain, Bree, 22, 43

Dessen, Sarah, 77

DiCamillo, Kate, 77, 111, 113

Dobry, 97

Dominic, 63

Dragon Castle, 35

Dragon of Og, The, 38

Draper, Sharon M., 79

*Dream Keeper and Other Poems,
    The:* "Dreams," 138

Dreamer, The, 129

Dreamers, 132

du Bois, William Pène, 42

Dumplin', 121

Duyvis, Corinne, 94

Each Kindness, 4

Edwards, Julie Andrews, 52

El Deafo, 78

Elatsoe, 43

Ella Enchanted, 70

Elliott, Zetta, 6, 121

Emperor Mage, 47, 69

*End of the Beginning: Being the
    Adventures of a Small Snail
    (and an Even Smaller Ant), The*, 45

Ende, Michael, 9, 34, 130

Engle, Margarita, 127

Enright, Elizabeth, 104

Erdrich, Louise, 136

*Ersatz Elevator, The
    (A Series of Unfortunate
    Events, Book the Sixth)*, 14

Esperanza Rising, 119

*Everything Sad Is Untrue
    (A True Story)*, 138

Fables, 72

Fancy Nancy, 87

Farizan, Sara, 115

Farmer, Nancy, 3, 74, 90, 96

Fault in Our Stars, The, 61

Feed, 53

Fellowship of the Ring, The, 127

Fifteen, 22

Finn Family Moomintroll, 38

First Rule of Punk, The, 66

147

Fish in a Tree, 79

Fitzhugh, Louise, 49, 96

Five Children and It, 46

Five Go off in a Caravan, 76

Flake, Sharon, 11, 120

*Flora and Ulysses:
    The Illuminated Adventures*, 111

Florian, Douglas, 99

Fly by Night, 72, 76

For Every One, 134

Forman, Gayle, 16

Freeman, Don, 81

Front Desk, 32, 64

Further Tales of Mr. Pengachoosa,
    19, 51

Gabi, a Girl in Pieces, 113

Gaiman, Neil, 12, 20, 35

Gansworth, Eric, 91, 112

Gantos, Jack, 63

Gay-Neck, the Story of a Pigeon, 15

Genesis Begins Again, 90

*George and Martha: The Complete
    Stories of Two Best Friends:
    "Split Pea Soup,"* 89

Ghost, 124

Ghost Boys, 66

Ghost of Spirit Bear, 110

Gift for Tía Rosa, A, 6

Gino, Alex, 120

Giovanni, Nikki, 32

Giraffes Can't Dance, 57

Girl Who Drank the Moon, The, 88

*Girl Who Fell Beneath Fairyland
    and Led the Revels There, The*, 24

Gleitzman, Morris, 114

Godden, Rumer, 38

Going Bovine, 109

Goldilocks and the Three Dinosaurs,
    37, 72

Goodbye Stranger, 42

Grandma's Bag of Stories, 96

Gratz, Alan, 55

Graveyard Book, The, 12

Great and Terrible Beauty, A, 23

Green, John, 61, 79

Greenwitch, 75

*Grim Grotto, The
    (A Series of Unfortunate
    Events, Book the Eleventh)*, 77

Hamilton, Virginia, 45, 97

Hammonds Reed, Christina, 34, 92

Han, Jenny, 39, 114

Hardinge, Frances, 72, 76, 97, 117,
    124

Harriet the Spy, 49, 96

*Harry Potter and the Half-Blood
    Prince*, 23

Harvey Potter's Balloon Farm, 9

Hate U Give, The, 115, 129

Heaven to Betsy, 19, 135

Henkes, Kevin, 12, 48, 111

Here We Are: Feminism for the Real World, 17

Here, There Be Dragons, 40

Herrera, Juan Felipe, 56

Hiranandani, Veera, 34, 37

Ho, Joanna, 35

Hoban, Russell, 20, 39

Hobbit, The, 39

Holes, 101, 116

Home of the Brave, 37

House of the Scorpion, The, 74, 90, 96

How Do You Live?, 121

How I Became a Ghost, 118

How Tía Lola Came to ~~Visit~~ Stay, 139

How Tía Lola Saved the Summer, 116

Howl's Moving Castle, 42, 71

Hughes, Langston, 102, 138

Hundred and One Dalmatians, The, 100

Hunt, Lynda Mullaly, 79, 122

I Am Malala: How One Girl Stood Up for Education and Changed the World, 15

I Am Not Your Perfect Mexican Daughter, 131

I'll Ask You Three Times, Are You OK?, 28

I'll Give You the Sun, 85

If I Ever Get Out of Here, 91

If You Could Be Mine, 115

Ihimaera, Witi, 104

Insectlopedia: Poems and Paintings, 99

Inside Out and Back Again, 86

Instructions, 20

Instructions for Dancing, 55, 90, 118

Invisible Life of Addie LaRue, The, 40

Ivy + Bean Make the Rules, 54

Jacob Have I Loved, 67

Jansson, Tove, 38, 41, 46, 71

Jennifer Chan Is Not Alone, 105, 133

Jensen, Kelly, 17

Joey Pigza Swallowed the Key, 63

Johnson, Angela, 46

Johnson, George M., 97

Johnson, Leah, 123

Johnson, Varian, 138

Jones, Diana Wynne, 4, 42, 71, 124

Juliet Takes a Breath, 122

Jumbies, The, 109

Junonia, 48

Just One Day, 16

Juster, Norton, 64, 75

Kadohata, Cynthia, 105

Kalman, Maira, 134

Keller, Helen, 64, 73

Keller, Tae, 35, 68, 77, 105, 133

Kelly, Erin Entrada, 131

Khan, Sabina, 125

Khorram, Adib, 115

King of Attolia, The, 93, 131

Kingdom on the Waves, The, 6

Kira-Kira, 105

Konigsberg, E. L., 80, 90

Kuskin, Karla, 101

L'Engle, Madeleine, 70, 126

Labyrinth Lost, 44

Lai, Thanhha, 86

Landy, Derek, 73

Last Night at the Telegraph Club, 87

Last of the Really Great Whangdoodles, The, 52

Last Stop on Market Street, 111

Laughing at My Nightmare, 30

Leaf, Munro, 106

Lentil, 56

Lester, Julius, 3, 61, 112

Levine, Gail Carson, 70

Lewis, C. S., vii, 13, 49, 78

Library, A, 32

Lie Tree, The, 97, 117

Lightning Dreamer: Cuba's Greatest Abolitionist, The, 127

Lightning Thief, The (Percy Jackson and the Olympians, Book One), 54

Lilly's Purple Plastic Purse, 111

Lin, Grace, 5, 110

Lindstrom, Carole, 103

List of Things That Will Not Change, The, 73

Little & Lion, 12

Little Badger, Darcie, 43

Little Engine That Could, The, 116

Little Prince, The, 106

Little Princess, A, 5, 27

Little Town on the Prairie, 66

Little White Bird, or Adventures in Kensington Gardens, The, 6

Little Women, 54

Lo, Malinda, 11, 87, 139

Lobel, Arnold, 31, 44, 72

Long Walk to Water, A, 118

Lost Conspiracy, The, 124

Loud Silence of Francine Green, The, 81

Love and Lies of Rukhsana Ali, The, 125

Lovelace, Maud Hart, 19, 117, 135

Lowry, Lois, 13, 92

M.C. Higgins, the Great, 45

MacLachlan, Patricia, 104

Mafi, Tahereh, 36

Magic World, The: "The Aunt and Amabel," 31

Magician's Nephew, The, 13, 78

Magoon, Kekla, 125

Makoons, 136

Marshall, James, 89

Marzipan Pig, The, 20

Mathers, Petra, 115

Matilda, 19

Max Makes a Million, 134

Mbalia, Kwame, 28

McCaughrean, Geraldine, 46, 53

McCloskey, Robert, 56

McKinley, Robin, 91, 98, 118

McKissack, Patricia, 112

Medina, Meg, 136

Melleby, Nicole, 87

Merci Suárez Changes Gears, 136

Midwife's Apprentice, The, 18

Mikaelsen, Ben, 98, 110

Milne, A. A., 69

Mistletoe and Murder, 40

Monster Calls, A, 76

Monsters of Men, 128

Montgomery, L. M., 22, 109

Moore, David Barclay, 128

Morales, Yuyi, 132

Mouse and His Child, The, 101

Mr. Galliano's Circus, 126

Mukerji, Dhan Gopal, 15

Murphy, Julie, 121

Murty, Sudha, 96

My Heart and Other Black Holes, 122

My Mama Says There Aren't Any Zombies, Ghosts, Vampires, Creatures, Demons, Monsters, Fiends, Goblins, or Things, 88

Myers, Walter Dean, 4

Mysterious Edge of the Heroic World, The, 80

Nayeri, Daniel, 138

Naylor, Phyllis Reynolds, 8, 73

Nelson, Jandy, 85

Nelson, Marilyn, 62

Nesbit, E., 31, 33, 46, 91

Ness, Patrick, 76, 128

Neverending Story, The, 9, 34, 130

New Kid, 94

Night Diary, The, 34, 37

Niven, Jennifer, 7

Nolen, Jerdine, 9

Number the Stars, 13

Nuts to You, 36

Nye, Naomi Shihab, 28

O'Connor, Jane, 87

Ogress and the Orphans, The, 4

Okorafor, Nnedi, 32, 51, 55, 68, 80, 105, 130

Olive's Ocean, 12

On Stories, and Other Essays on Literature, vii

On the Edge of Gone, 94

Once Was a Time, 53

One and Only Ivan, The, 98

One Came Home, 10

One Crazy Summer, 51, 121, 132

One for the Murphys, 122

Other Words for Home, 7, 16

Out of My Mind, 79

Owen, James A., 40

Palacio, R. J., xi, 68

Parachutes, 42

Park, Linda Sue, 24, 30, 118

Parker Inheritance, The, 138

Parr, Maria, 62

Paterson, Katherine, 67, 93

Pax, 87, 122

Peace, Locomotion, 28

Peck, Richard, 85, 94

Pennypacker, Sara, 87, 122

Pérez, Celia C., 66

Perkins, Lynne Rae, 36

Perkins, Mitali, 33

Phantom Tollbooth, The, 64, 75

Piecing Me Together, 17

Pierce, Tamora, 47, 69, 91

Piper, Watty, 116

Pla, Sally J., 69

Planet of Junior Brown, The, 97

Poet X, The, 120

Polar Express, The, 134

Popcorn: Poems: "The Bakery," 38

Potter, Beatrix, 52

Pratchett, Terry, 96

Princess on the Brink, 51

Pullman, Philip, 47

Punching the Air, 135

Quintero, Isabel, 113

Railway Children, The, 91

Ramona and Her Father, 86

Ramona Forever, 8

Ramona the Brave, 51, 113

Raskin, Ellen, 50

Reaper at the Gates, A, 36

Refugee, 55

Return to Gone-Away, 104

Reynolds, Jason, 124, 134

Rhodes, Jewell Parker, 66

Rick, 120

Ringgold, Faith, 136

Riordan, Rick, 54

Rivera, Gabby, 122

Rivera, Lilliam, 88

Roar and More, 101

Rock and the River, The, 125

Roll of Thunder, Hear My Cry, 126

Rooftoppers, 33

Rose in Bloom, 20

Rosetown Summer, 99

Rowling, J. K., 23

Rundell, Katherine, 33, 56

Rush, Caroline, 19, 51
Ryan, Pam Muñoz, 119, 129
Rylant, Cynthia, 99
Sachar, Louis, 30, 101, 116
Saeed, Aisha, 13, 114, 128
Sáenz, Benjamin Alire, 3, 62, 105
Saint-Exupéry, Antoine de, 106
Salaam, Yusef, 135
Sales, Leila, 53
Sánchez, Erika L., 131
Sarah, Plain and Tall, 104
Say Her Name, 6
Schwab, V. E., 40
Science of Being Angry, The, 87
Scieszka, Jon, 110
Scorpions, 4
Sea of Trolls, The, 3
Secrets at Sea, 85
Selden, George, 71
Sendak, Maurice, 27
Sepetys, Ruta, 94
Seth, Vikram, 101
Shannon, David, 47
Shannon, Monica, 97
*Sideways Stories from
  Wayside School*, 30
Silence that Binds Us, The, 35
Silent to the Bone, 90
Silver Chair, The, 49, 62

Silver on the Tree, 8, 132
Single Shard, A, 30
Skim, 66
Skin I'm In, The, 11, 120
Skulduggery Pleasant, 73
Smith, Amber, 24
Smith, Dodie, 100
Snicket, Lemony, 14, 63, 77
Snyder, Zilpha Keatley, 49, 102, 133
So Totally Emily Ebers, 9
Someday Birds, The, 69
Something Beautiful, 27
Sotomayor, Sonia, 33
Spindle's End, 91
Stars Beneath Our Feet, The, 128
Stead, Rebecca, 42, 73, 114
Steig, William, 63
Stevens, Robin, 40
Stevenson, James, 38
*Stinky Cheese Man and Other Fairly
  Stupid Tales, The*, 110
Stone, Nic, 78
Story of Ferdinand, The, 106
Story of My Life, The, 64, 73
Streatfeild, Noel, 50
Summer Book, The, 71
Summer to Die, A, 92
Sun Is Also a Star, The, 74
Sweet and Sour Animal Book, The, 102

Sweet Far Thing, The, 52

Symphony for the City of the Dead: Dmitri Shostakovich and the Siege of Leningrad, 61

Taha, Karen T., 6

Tahir, Sabaa, 36, 56

Tale of Despereaux, The, 113

Tale of Little Pig Robinson, The, 52

Tale of the Mandarin Ducks, The, 93

Tales from Moominvalley, 41

Tamaki, Mariko, 66

Tar Beach, 136

Taylor, Mildred D., 126

Then, 114

Thirsty, 119

Thomas, Angie, 115, 129

Three Keys, 89

Timberlake, Amy, 10

Tin Princess, The, 47

Tingle, Tim, 118

To All the Boys I've Loved Before, 39

Tolkien, J. R. R., 39, 127

Touching Spirit Bear, 98

Tough Guide to Fantasyland, The, 124

Truth about Forever, The, 77

Tuck Everlasting, 50, 135

Turner, Megan Whalen, 93, 131

Turning Pages: My Life Story, 33

Twenty-One Balloons, The, 42

Unravel Me, 36

Valente, Catherynne M., 24

Van Allsburg, Chris, 134

Very Hungry Caterpillar, The, 41

Victor and Christabel, 115

Viorst, Judith, 11, 88

Voting Booth, The, 129

Waiting for You, 23

Warga, Jasmine, 7, 16, 122

Waterless Mountain, 99

Watson, Renée, 17

Way I Used to Be, The, 24

We Are Water Protectors: "Earth Steward and Water Protector Pledge," 103

We'll Always Have Summer, 114

Wee Free Men, The, 96

Westing Game, The, 50

Whale Rider, The, 104

What Is Given from the Heart, 112

When Dad Killed Mom, 61, 112

When My Name Was Keoko, 24

When You Reach Me, 114

When You Trap a Tiger, 35, 68, 77

Where the Mountain Meets the Moon, 5, 110

Where the Wild Things Are, 27

Whiskers and Rhymes: "Books to the Ceiling," 31

White Darkness, The, 46, 53

White, E. B., 89

Who Fears Death, 105

Wilder, Laura Ingalls, 66

Will Sparrow's Road, 117

Willems, Mo, 37, 72

Williams-Garcia, Rita, 57, 121, 132

Williams, Alicia, 90

Winnie-the-Pooh, 69

Wish After Midnight, A, 121

Wishtree, 93

Witches of Worm, The, 133

With the Fire on High, 18

Wolf Hollow, 14

Wolf Wilder, The, 56

Wolk, Lauren, 14

Wonder, 68

Wonderful Garden, The, 33

Wonderful Wizard of Oz, The, 74, 85

Woo Hoo! You're Doing Great!, 20

Woodson, Jacqueline, 4, 28, 36, 80, 133

Wrinkle in Time, A, 70, 126

Written in the Stars, 114

Wyeth, Sharon Dennis, 27

Yang, Kelly, 32, 42, 64, 89

Year Down Yonder, A, 94

Yee, Lisa, 9

Yep, Laurence, 14

Yoon, Nicola, 55, 74, 90, 118

Yoshino, Genzaburō, 121

You Bring the Distant Near, 33

You Go First, 131

You Should See Me in a Crown, 123

Yousafzai, Malala, 15

Zahrah the Windseeker, 51

Zoboi, Ibi, 135